THE SUMMER HOUSE

THE SUMMER HOUSE

LAKESIDE COTTAGES, SEASIDE RETREATS, AND COUNTRY IDYLLS

~ JACI CONRY ~

RIZZOLI
NEW YORK

New York · Paris · London · Milan

CONTENTS

INTRODUCTION

SUMMER HOUSE: THESE TWO WORDS EVOKE A SENSE OF NOSTALGIA, a twinge of romance, and a sigh of relaxation. The screen door open to the breeze off the lake. Sunbeams crossing a cheerfully painted floor. A simple coverlet on a wood-framed bed, with views of the sea beyond. Mismatched china piled high on open kitchen shelves. It's sand perpetually on bare feet, on the wood floors, and in bed. It's grilling and fresh seafood, strawberries, and potato salad. Lakes and swimming pools, hikes and beach walks. Naps in front of the fan.

Summer houses come with their own set of sounds, too. There's the thunk of the screen door when it closes and the slight creak from the hinges as it opens. The whirring of a boat motor as it pulls away from the dock. The gentle lapping of ocean waves. A nighttime chorus of crickets. A summer house is a state of mind, a place of respite, where the boundaries between indoor and outdoor living are blurred, where you can step away from the complexities and frenetic pace of daily existence, if only for a few days.

Even if you don't have your own summer home or have easy access to someone else's, chances are you've at least been to one and have memories of a carefree time spent there. Or you have an inkling, a sense gleaned from others or from books and movies, of the rituals associated with one: the first dip in the ocean, swimming to the raft at the center of the lake, an annual clambake, beach picnics,

Opposite: Shades of blue, pops of red, and a variety of check patterns make this generational family retreat in coastal Maine, designed by Lilse McKenna, sing.

bike rides, and casual badminton games on a fraying net set up on the lawn.

Summer homes emerged in the United States with the development of railroads and steamships and the growing wealth of the upper class. Toward the end of the nineteenth century, it became easier to travel to remote areas and those with the budget to do so packed up and fled from heat-sapped cities to lakeside enclaves, beach towns, or the mountains. They traveled with entourages, too—extended family members, servants, elaborate wardrobes, and large quantities of silver and fine china. Sometimes they even brought their favorite furnishings along for the season.

The most lavish summer "cottages" were built during the Gilded Age by wealthy industrialists in Newport, Rhode Island. There, the Astors, Morgans, and Vanderbilts spent the season in ornate residences that took design cues from European palaces. Elite Bostonians and New Yorkers also flocked to the cool climate of the Berkshires, where lauded architecture firms like McKim, Mead & White and Peabody & Sterns designed gracious, if slightly less extravagant than the manses of their Newport counterparts, estates for notables, including novelist Edith Wharton. Another prominent summer colony of the era was Bar Harbor, Maine, where many sprawling Queen Anne and shingle-style homes built at the turn of the twentieth century still stand proudly today. While much socializing and entertaining took place at these splendid homes, residents focused their days on enjoying family and friends, as well as the outdoors: swimming and sailing, playing tennis and golf, and strolling amid refreshing sea breezes, following a calmer pace than their typical day-to-day lives allowed.

By the end of World War I, the grandeur of the Gilded Age had faded, signaling the end of such costly summer getaways. The concept of laid-back summer living was all but inconceivable as the Great Depression and World War II took hold. By the late 1940s and 1950s, though, there was a summer house revival, buoyed by a new surge of economic prosperity. Increasingly Americans sought second homes—far smaller and simpler than their grand predecessors—as

Opposite: Upon stepping through the front door of this family home in Seal Harbor, you see all the way through the house to the back, where an expansive deck with a panoramic view of the harbor and adjacent islands sits.

escapes on the coast, in wooded settings, and near the mountains. Over the ensuing decades, Newport's summer population swelled again, along with that of Maine's resort communities and those on Cape Cod, Martha's Vineyard, and Nantucket in Massachusetts. By the 1970s, the hamlets, towns, and villages of the Hamptons rose in popularity as a seasonal retreat, and those who favored a slower pace found their way to time-honored camps in the Catskills and Adirondacks. While this later crop of summer house dwellers was less flashy than the early industrialists on their vast estates, their desires were the same: to connect with outdoors and their loved ones, to slow down, and to cool off.

Most of us, I think, crave the simplicity of loose, unscheduled summer days. Unplugging from our ever-present "on" switch is harder now than it has ever been before, and that makes the essence of a summer house all the more precious. It's been a delight to create this book. On the following pages, we celebrate every sort of summer house—from the quaint and cozy to the more polished; from the spare to those overflowing with lore and relics. There are lake cabins and island hideaways; secret spots and beach houses; and homes on bustling main streets and cottages nestled in the woods. There are antique homes with well-loved patina, while others are newly built, fine-tuned, and tailored. These places are beloved by the people who live in them, revered by the architects and designers who work on them, and deeply appreciated by the families and friends who have the occasion to visit. It is the collective stories of their inhabitants that give life to these homes. I'm ever grateful that these narratives were shared with me.

Opposite: Jewelry designer Brent Neale Winston—who worked on the design of her summer residence with her sister, Ramsey Lyons—and her family take as many summer meals as possible out in the garden.

PROVINCETOWN, MASSACHUSETTS

PERFECTLY IMPERFECT

KEN FULK FIRST VISITED PROVINCETOWN IN 1991, WHEN A FRIEND brought him down from Boston, where he was living at the time. As they drove into the town, situated at the outermost tip of Cape Cod, Fulk recalls feeling "that love at first sight sensation." Surrounded on three sides by water, nestled in the sand dunes, 90 percent of Provincetown is contained within the Cape Cod National Seashore. "It's a deeply beautiful place," says Fulk, who is renowned for creating bold, bespoke, utterly to-the-max interiors and out-of-this-world experiences.

That awe-inspiring, unspoiled nature of the landscape aside, what he finds most precious about the town is the fact that "everyone you love is within arm's reach here. It's such a tiny place that you see your friends twice a day as you're riding your bike around. There are impromptu pop-ins all day long at my house," Fulk says. He notes that he and his husband, Kurt Wootton, have a wonderful life in New York City and in California, "but seeing friends takes lots of planning in those places, which is fine. But it's different here and we really treasure that. Everyone who lives here feels this way and there's such energy, a joy and goodness, that comes out of it."

The region is the ancestral land of the Wampanoag people, who farmed and fished. Sadly, their population was decimated by diseases brought by Europeans. It is common knowledge that the Pilgrims first landed in Provincetown in 1620 on their way to Plymouth. It's less widely known that the town was previously visited

Opposite: Fulk says that his dogs consider this cozy room overlooking the sea their own. The ceiling, trim, and walls are all painted in Benjamin Moore Dash of Curry.

in 1602 by English settlers led by explorer Bartholomew Gosnold, who named the area that is now Provincetown Cape Cod for the vast schools of codfish that he encountered there. The fishing village was officially incorporated as a township in 1727, and it went on to experience prosperity as a whaling port. By the early twentieth century, the town established itself as an arts and culture haven.

With fewer than four thousand year-round residents, Provincetown's population can swell to sixty thousand in July and August. "In summer, there is such a delightful mix of people here," says Fulk. "Nowhere else can you find an eight-foot-tall drag queen, a family with a chubby kid eating taffy, a grizzly old Yankee, and a Portuguese fishing crew all sitting in the same stew."

After he and Wootton bought their first home in Provincetown's East End in 2007, Fulk became drawn to a forlorn-looking house that he frequently passed on Commercial Street, the town's main drag. The house was owned by a collector who'd filled the rooms with so much stuff that it was literally sagging under the weight of it all. "The porches were overflowing, weighted down with junk, and the back of the house was held up with a car jack," Fulk recalls. "But I would look at it and think, 'What a wonderful, old house.'"

In 2012, Fulk and Wootton purchased the crumbling, Victorian-style cottage. Overlooking Provincetown Harbor and beyond to Long Point, it had been built in 1905 for the town's first electrician, during a time when living on the water was just becoming desirable. There's no question that the house was withering when Fulk took ownership, but he approached renovations with considerable trepidation. "We've watched a lot of houses here have their architecture wiped away as changes were made to adapt them for the lives of new owners," he says. "And that was a real concern to us. We were determined to keep the physical nature that time and place had had on the structure."

While installing new electrical and heating systems were a necessity, Fulk opted to preserve the original small rooms. He retained the narrow hallway, the original plaster walls, and the kitchen's scant footprint and blue painted floors. Some cosmetic decisions were forced, like in the dining room where the original plaster was "rotting off the wall," he says, which led to the creation of the hand-drawn mural depicting Old Provincetown. The room's built-in hutch with peeling paint is original. It houses colored glassware, antique silverware, an array of dishes from transferware to fine porcelain, and everything in between. "Some of it is fanciful, some are from flea markets," says Fulk, noting that he and Wootton draw from the treasured collection for their everyday dishes. "We bring it all out to the dock when we have parties out there, too. If you have something you love, you should use it as much as possible."

The home's wraparound, double-deck porches were added in the 1940s, and a window seat was a later installation. When the home was a boardinghouse in the 1960s, the six bedroom doors had numbers added to them, and they're still there. "When local people come to the house, they say, 'This is old P-town' and that's what I wanted so deeply," says Fulk.

The furnishings weren't bought with "great, deep intention," says Fulk. Pieces came from Brimfield Antique Flea Market, antique markets in London, and Eldred's, the Cape's sole auction house. Some things have interesting pedigrees, such as a bed with a rounded canopy that belonged to news correspondent Diane Sawyer and her director husband, Mike Nichols. Before the famous couple owned it, the bed was in one of Marjorie Merriweather Post's residences, where it belonged to her daughter, actress Dina Merrill.

The walls of the second-floor hallway are adorned with dog portraits, which Fulk, who has four beloved pups, has long collected. "I often make these great family photo walls in the more private areas of houses, and this one is similar," he says. "It was important to me to do everything myself in the house, and I hung these portraits freestyle. When I see this tribute hall to these creatures who enrich our lives, it's hard not to bring a smile to my face."

This summer home's patina, weathered appeal, slanted floors, and chipped paint can be surprising to some houseguests. "They think they are coming to a posh beach house," laughs Fulk. "But no, it's my crooked house by the sea. The bathroom is down the hall and the shower is outside. 'If that appeals to you,' I tell them, 'come visit!'"

To Fulk, the allure of this quite lovely but undoubtedly touched-by-time house is simple. "In my life, I create extravagant things. This is so not that," he says. Every year, he brings his design team to Provincetown to experience what he calls Designing in the Dunes. "One of the reasons why I do this is to show them that luxury isn't just about what things cost. It can be the simplest things, the utterly imperfect, that are the most precious."

Left: The side porch, oriented toward the garden, provides a pleasing place to take shelter from the sun.

Above: Pots and knives are stored in plain sight on the kitchen's beadboard walls, contributing to the home's collected feel. *Opposite*: The kitchen opens to a wonderful sunporch, overlooking the garden and harbor, where Fulk and Wootton spend much of their time. *Overleaf*: While the original plaster in the dining room had to be removed, Fulk was able to salvage the trim. The colored glassware is from Fulk's collection.

Opposite: New kitchen cabinets on one wall were locally crafted and painted in Farrow & Ball Tanner's Brown. *Above*: The hutch contains an array of beautiful china collected by Fulk over decades. *Overleaf left*: In the front hall, the early twentieth-century campaign chest and the portrait to the left of it are Brimfield Antiques Show finds. *Overleaf right*: The lower-level bathroom features a rare peg leg sink. The walls are covered in a Colefax and Fowler paper featuring soft pink tree peonies, one of Fulk's favorites.

Opposite: The second-floor hallway is lined with portraits of dogs that Fulk has picked up over the years. *Above*: The canopy bed was originally used in Majorie Merriweather Post's Adirondack Camp, Camp Topridge, by her daughter, Dina Merrill. Before Fulk bought it, the bed was in the Connecticut country home of Diane Sawyer and Mike Nichols.

Above: In the upstairs bathroom, a vintage wicker hamper resembling a penguin is used as a wastebasket. *Opposite*: In the primary bedroom, the custom bed is draped in an unlined, striped Rose Tarlow linen fabric. *Overleaf*: The back of the home faces the harbor where Fulk and Wootten's dogs swim daily—Fulk himself takes a dip almost as often.

LOCUST VALLEY, NEW YORK

SISTER STORY

In 2019, when jewelry designer Brent Neale Winston first saw Hay Fever, a stately three-story home amid two lush acres in Locust Valley, New York, she fell a little bit in love. But even though the house, which dates back to 1668, was on the market, she wasn't ready for it. The Manhattan mom of three and her husband, Michael Winston, weren't thinking about buying a second home yet.

Come June 2020, however, the young family found themselves in a different mindset. "[We were] holed up at my sister's weekend house outside of Pittsburgh wondering what was going to happen to the world," recalls Winston. "We called and made an offer on the house so fast." Just like that, the home was theirs.

There's a timeless quality to Locust Valley, located in Oyster Bay in Nassau County. Homes are shaded by centuries-old trees, and there are land preserves, botanical gardens, and a grand, yellow firehouse topped with a cupola. From Hay Fever, it's a short stroll to the village proper—a small downtown dotted with antique stores, boutiques, a pizza place, and a coffee shop. But back at the house, where Winston and her family, along with her parents, now spend the summer months, "you have no idea you're in the middle of town. It feels so calm, like you've escaped," she says.

Built by one of the town's settlers, Captain John Underhill, the home is a mix of styles, including Dutch Colonial and Colonial Revival elements that mark

Opposite: Family meals are often enjoyed outdoors in the courtyard, and it's also a favorite spot for entertaining. The Julia Amory tablecloth is paired with vintage green chairs.

the various eras of the house. It was a Quaker boys' school in the 1840s, later a museum and restaurant, and, through the centuries, home to several families, including the Wyckoffs, who gave the home the moniker "Hay Fever" after the Noël Coward play about an eccentric family hosting weekend guests at their English country house. Updates were made to the structure in the eighteenth century and then again in the 1920s, when the house was expanded to connect with the outbuildings on the left and right, creating a U-shape—which is the aspect that Winston finds most appealing. "The kitchen is off the courtyard, the main hallway is off the courtyard, and my bedroom is too," she says. "Access to the outside is everywhere and because of that, the outside is really brought into the house."

Before the place could truly feel like home for the family, much work had to be done inside. The home had been previously owned by decorator Jeffrey Bilhuber, who had completed a significant renovation that involved the overhaul of the home's systems. While the rooms had been beautifully decorated, the vibe was a bit more formal than what Winston had in mind. To fine-tune the design, she looked no further than the sister she was braving out the pandemic with, interior designer Ramsey Lyons. "I would never hire anyone else," laughs Winston. "Ramsey understands our family dynamic and how we use spaces. She knows I want the house to look a certain way, that I love color and texture, without me having to tell her."

Indeed Lyons agrees, adding that she and Winston gravitate to similar aesthetics in both what they wear and how they decorate their homes. In some cases, though, she had to encourage Winston to veer outside of her comfort zone. "I would say, 'You may not love it right now, but let's try it and give it some time; if you don't like it, we can take it out.' None of those things came out," recalls Lyons. She also notes that the decor evolved over two years. "We weren't in a rush; we kept adding layers. We didn't have to execute the design so quickly and I think that helped us avoid making mistakes."

Given that part of the house is 350 years old, there are quite a few quirks about it. The wide-plank wood floors are slanted, rooms are oddly shaped, every room is a pass-through, and every window in the house is crooked. While customizing upholstery and window treatments took extra consideration because of these characteristics—a skirted bench in the family room, for example, has three different size legs so it doesn't wobble on the slopping floor—the home's original details, including many of the doors, the fireplace surrounds, and nineteenth-century windows, are cherished.

The home sings with pink, green, and red hues, and bold, playful patterns fill rooms with vibrancy and movement. "It's a fun house," says Winston, noting that her children's artwork hangs on the walls along with pieces by renowned contemporary artists. Most of the furniture are antiques from various eras, though nothing is too precious. "My kids are young. They are hard on stuff so everything here can withstand them," says Winston. She invited her nine-year-old twin girls to be involved in the design of their room; they requested princess beds. And while the room does indeed have beds with enchanting canopies in Schumacher fabric and a lively Pierre Frey wallcovering that emulates a woodsy motif, the vibe isn't too young. "It was important that the color scheme be mature enough to grow with them," says Winston. As much as she loves the girls' room, however, Winston considers her and Michael's bedroom to be her favorite part of the house. "There's just so much space for things. Coming from an apartment in the city, that's a real luxury. There's a whole seating area and a fireplace, the kids come in and watch movies with us. It's heaven."

Of course, most of their time at Hay Fever is spent outdoors. "We don't have a yard in the city so it's magical to have all this outdoor space. For the kids, they live differently here; they love all the freedom they get to have," says Winston, who enjoys hosting alfresco dinner parties, gatherings by the pool, and friendly ping-pong matches on the porch. "There's just a wonderful energy to the house, and you notice it as soon as you arrive. It envelops you."

❋

Overleaf left: Among the most charming attributes of the seventeenth-century house's exterior are the misaligned windows. *Overleaf right*: The steep, narrow stairway leads to the second floor.

Right: The living room is painted in two shades of blue; the wall above the chair rail is Benjamin Moore Palladian Blue, while the wall below is Benjamin Moore Stratton Blue. The armchair and ottoman are upholstered in lively Pierre Frey fabric.

Opposite: An antique dining table is paired with chairs reupholstered in Pierre Frey fabric, and another Pierre Frey pattern sheaths the walls. *Above*: The inside of the built-in cabinet was painted red by the previous homeowner Jeffery Bilhuber—one of the design elements that Winston kept. *Overleaf*: In the kitchen, open shelves display dishware without impeding the view of the yard.

Above: The trim and bookshelves in the library are painted in sultry Benjamin Moore Sultan's Palace; the wallpaper on the ceiling is Schumacher. *Opposite*: A custom skirted banquette sits along a corner of the family room, where dark wood walls create an enveloping feel.

Below: In a guest bathroom, both the walls and ceiling are covered in a vibrant, whimsical Pierre Frey motif. *Right*: In the daughters' room, romantic canopies made of Schumacher fabric evoke the feel of princess beds. Winston also made sure that the wallcovering could grow with the girls.

Overleaf left: The primary bedroom, where the walls are sheathed in vibrant Quadrille print, is one of Winston's favorite spaces in the house. *Overleaf right*: In the primary bathroom, the vanity, tub surround, and trim are painted in Benjamin Moore Jamestown Blue; the wallpaper is Schumacher.

SUTTON ISLAND, MAINE

SECRET SPLENDOR

NATURE IS UTTERLY UNBLEMISHED ON SUTTON ISLAND. HERE, there are no paved roads, no cars, and no year-round residents. Walking paths traverse the semiwild terrain. There are cobble beaches, rock formations, and only twenty homes. One of the Cranberry Isles located south of Mount Desert Island in Maine, the one-mile-long Sutton Island is largely a secret, a place you'd never know exists unless you're lucky enough to have roots there, like Nadia Rosenthal does.

Rosenthal spent the summers of her childhood traipsing across the island with her sister. Curious, independent, and creative, the girls made art and jewelry out of shells and stones in the house that they have since inherited from their parents. Today, Rosenthal and her husband spend every summer here. Rambling with weathered gray shingles, the house looks remarkably well preserved for a place built 125 years ago and then abandoned—left for dead for a decade, with a pantry full of Waterford crystal, bookcases crammed with first editions, and the table set for dinner.

The story of this beloved home, raised up on a bluff whose view across the lawn is of Acadia National Park and beyond to the deep, blue ocean, started in 1899 when William Burnham, an heir to a steam-locomotive fortune in Philadelphia, purchased a quarter of the island as an escape for his family from the steamy city summers. "There was an extraordinary social scene here in the late nineteenth century," says Rosenthal. "Burnham and his wife, Emma, built

Opposite: The house clad in cedar shingles is steps from the rocky shoreline.

this house and two others on either side for extended family." The family traveled by rail—with a second car for their Irish servants—and then by steamship from Philadelphia to reach their destination every summer.

The home's floors, ceilings, and walls were clad with cypress, known for its resistance to moisture, grown in the swamps of Georgia. The Burnhams' summers were very formal, according to Rosenthal. "We have photos of the women sitting on the huge porches wearing hats with mosquito netting, with maids bringing out food in huge tureens," she says.

In the 1920s, one of the Burnhams' nephews and his family moved into the house. They set about making renovations, some of which were unfortunate. In their effort to deformalize the architecture, a shed dormer was put on the front of the house and a gracious balcony was removed. The new inhabitants sought to fill the house with music and brought in two pianos, one of which was a striking, rare 1864 Steinway concert grand piano made of Brazilian rosewood. To accommodate the pianos in the same space, a porch was taken over to expand the living room. Despite the effort they put into the place, the family's tenure in the home was cut short: after a beloved son died in World War II, they abandoned the house and everything in it. "They just left the original Stickley furniture, pianos, the butler's pantry full of crystal and Wedgewood, and exotic porcelain tea sets," says Rosenthal. "And never returned."

For over ten years, the house sat empty. By the time it was sold for one dollar to a couple of actors who were part of a summer stock theater in the area, winters had taken a toll on the house. But it had survived, thanks to its construction on stilts, which protected it from the most extreme storm damage. "Since the house was aired from underneath, the wood didn't rot," says Rosenthal. The fact that the house is thirty-five feet above sea level saved the pianos. "They wouldn't have lasted anywhere else; pianos need to be in a constant humidity," she adds.

The actors fixed up the house, little by little. Rosenthal's family started renting it from the couple in 1955 right after her father came home from the Korean War. They fell in love with the house, eventually buying it and ten acres along the water for a mere $14,500—which she stresses was an enormous sum to her film composer father and mother at the time. "My dad spent years paying off the money they borrowed to buy the property, but it was worth it," says Rosenthal.

After visiting the home occasionally for four decades, Rosenthal and her sister inherited it several years ago. They began restoring the house, which had suffered a bit from the elements and limited funds over time, to its original glory. The nineteenth-century blueprints were unearthed in the attic and became a guide for the restoration. "The living room ceiling was sagging and our contractor discovered that several structural beams were missing. According to the blueprints, there were supposed to be these beams that just weren't there," recalls Rosenthal. "Most of the house was essentially being held up by the roof." Porches were put back where they belonged, and the shed dormer that Rosenthal always thought looked out of place was removed and replaced with a peak from the original plan. The house was reshingled, and a new roof and French drains were installed.

Now sturdy and sound for at least another century, the house stands proud. While it has no central heating, fireplaces ease the chilly late summer mornings and nights, and the kitchen has a Victorian wood-burning stove as it did when William and Emma Burnham were residents. Throughout, adjustments were made for contemporary living. Upstairs, for example, the sweeping hallway was condensed to allow the five bedrooms to be expanded. "People want bigger bedrooms now than when the house was built," says Rosenthal, noting that the house is filled with family all summer long. "Sometimes it's packed with people! But so much fun, everyone's exploring, eating, going down to the beach, just loving being here."

Against storms, solitude, and time, the house will remain a steadfast witness to generations of summer visitors.

❋

Overleaf: The home has no central heating, so it's not suitable for living during the cold months. This room, however, is toasty during early autumn thanks to the large fireplace.

Opposite: Tall, lovely windows and doors—even in the rooms that don't face the water—ensure that every space has an expansive connection to the outdoors. *Above*: An enclosed porch with a perfectly framed view of the sea offers a spot to settle when the winds pick up.

Left: When the house was passed on to Rosenthal and her sister, they embarked on a restoration while being careful to pay homage to its late nineteenth-century origins. The kitchen, for example, includes a nineteenth-century wood stove. *Overleaf left*: The original cabinets have seen nearly a century of use. *Overleaf right, clockwise from top left*: Copper bottom pots and wrought iron skillets are from various decades; a deep, antique soapstone sink still in tip-top shape; a glimpse of the ocean is visible through the trees from this small window at the back of the house.

Above and opposite: When the previous owners abandoned the house in the 1940s, they left all of its contents, including the cabinet full of china in the dining room. Miraculously, much of it has remained intact and is used by Rosenthal and her family today. *Overleaf*: In the living room, the rosewood piano stands side by side with the other nineteenth-century piano; both are still in beautiful playing condition.

Above: The bathrooms still have many of the original plumbing fixtures. *Right*: During the renovation, the home's five bedrooms were slightly expanded while retaining their historic detailing. *Overleaf*: In a twin bedroom, for example, the original cypress-clad walls and ceiling remain unchanged.

Opposite and above: What was once a sleeping porch is now a prime napping spot and an art studio with a view. *Overleaf*: On Sutton Island, walking paths serve as "streets" connecting various properties.

DARK HARBOR, MAINE

SUMMER HOUSE

THE JANUARY 1967 ISSUE OF *HOUSE & GARDEN* INCLUDED A FEATURE on Sister Parish's summer haven in Dark Harbor, a village located on the southernmost end of Islesboro, a small island near the center of Maine's Penobscot Bay, that dazzled decorators with its "undecorated look." It was noted in the article that cushioned ease was abundant throughout the nineteenth-century Cape: "One can sit or lie almost anywhere. . . . You can sit up, comfortably supported, straight as a poker, or in a child's rocker (if you can fit into it) or stretch out on the floor in front of any number of fireplaces. However oriented, you will always have something to look at. Parish does not believe in wasted space, barren corners, or lonely unadorned tables."

Dark Harbor was developed around the turn of the twentieth century as a summer retreat for families from New York, Philadelphia, and Boston. Parish, whose grandparents had a home on the island, spent her childhood summers there. She wrote, in an unpublished memoir, "I have never spent a summer out of the sight of my grandparents' house and the harbor and the hills and our ocean neighbors: Vinalhaven, North Haven, Deer Isle and the dozen little 'picnic islands' that dot Penobscot Bay. The view never changes, the island never changes, and the people hardly ever change."

Indeed, more than a century after Parish started coming to the area as a baby, the island remains virtually unchanged. There are a general store, a farmers market,

Opposite: Above a desk in the parlor hangs an oil portrait of Sister Parish's daughter, Apple Parish Bartlett, painted when she was a girl.

and a place to get ice cream. There's nothing pretentious about Dark Harbor: Summer residents picnic, swim, and sail; they play tennis and golf at the local club.

After Parish married, she and her husband, Harry, bought a canary-yellow house on the same point as her grandparents' property. Built in the early nineteenth century as a sea captain's cottage, the home had been added on to over the years, but it was far from a grand house, says Susan Crater, Parish's granddaughter. "It was perfectly situated, with a lawn gently rolling to the sea. They called it the Summer House." Crater and her mother, Apple (Parish's daughter), along with her children and grandchildren, and her brothers and their families, continue to spend time each summer on the island, enjoying the home that Parish cherished.

Parish was one of the grande dame decorators, whose client list included the names Vanderbilt, Whitney, Paley, Mellon, Getty, and Rockefeller. She joined with Albert Hadley to create the esteemed firm of Parish Hadley. Most famously, she decorated the Georgetown quarters of Senator John F. Kennedy and his wife, Jacqueline. When they moved to the White House, she adorned their private suites there. Eschewing trends or particular styles, Parish's trademark spaces had warmth and character that radiated from the array of patterns—some boldly colored, many of them chintz—and furniture—Anglo-American, Chippendale, and exotic wood pieces—that she paired together.

One of Parish's strictest tenets both for her clients and her own homes was that spaces lend themselves to comfortable conversation. In Maine, seating abounds. A photograph in *House & Garden* captures cushioned canvas banquettes on the porch heaped with pillows covered in a riot of fabrics designed by Hadley. The article states that "she lets colors fall where they may, and they always seem friendly." Mixing, rather than matching, was the venerable designer's secret to the undecorated look. At every turn, there is something to catch the eye, art of every type, porcelain figurines, and books. The house continues to evolve from one generation to the next, but the overall look set by Parish is largely unchanged. While part of that can be attributed to nostalgia, it's mostly because her family members share her sense of aesthetics.

Parish felt that a static house becomes tiresome, and the *House & Garden* article notes that "she changes something every day—usually by rearrangement, or more occasionally, a switch in the fabric. She rarely duplicates a pattern, preferring instead to play her 'mixing game' until she finds a tonic to keep the over-all setup in harmony in a new way. The house, consequently, is a bit like a kaleidoscope that is constantly given gentle little shakes to keep it on its toes." Crater and her daughter, Eliza, who run the heritage textile and wallcovering brand Sister Parish Design, treat the home as a design lab of sorts, thoughtfully incorporating new motifs from their collections into the decor. "We play with colors and textures, move furniture around," says Crater, adding that they hold photo shoots at the house, host their staff, and invite other designers to visit for inspiration, as Parish did.

One of the things Parish loved to do most, recalls Crater, was swim in the ocean. "At the foot of the lawn, there is a dark green lattice gazebo, which is used as a kind of bathhouse. There, Sister kept her worn D. Porthault terry cloth bathrobe with its faded pink initials "DMP," her white canvas Keds, which she used as swimming shoes, and her dark-blue, skirted swimsuit." After her swims, Parish would sit on the porch and conduct business by phone with her office in New York. "She spoke in whispered and dramatic expletives, her face painted with concern or impatience: 'You can't paint it green, it would be fatal' or 'I can't face it, Albert. You must fix it before I get back.'"

A champion of American crafts, Parish's summer retreat remains filled with the hallmarks of her iconic laid-back and layered styling: light-colored floral motifs, crocheted throws, quilts, needlepoint pillows, hand-hooked rugs, and rag rugs. Color is everywhere: there are painted floors and furniture, yellow walls, and blue ceilings. The dining room shelves are stocked with Dodie Thayer lettuce ware and other ceramic vegetables, collected by Parish. When she and Harry bought the house in the 1930s, they acquired one hundred pieces of golden oak furniture for one hundred dollars. She refreshed these items with white enamel and painted some with roses, vines, pine trees, cats, dogs, and birds; many of these furnishings remain in the house—ensuring that more than a generation later—Parish's essence continues to endure at her cherished Summer House.

Opposite: White-painted wrought iron furniture is arranged under the shaded canopy of trees at the edge of Dark Harbor. *Above*: The porch, with blue ceiling and chaises and armchairs, is among the home's most cherished gathering spots.

Right: In the front parlor, where a woven rag rug sits atop the spring-green floors, there are ample places to perch. *Overleaf*: The living room exudes a similar aesthetic with trompe l'oeil pelmets that were painted by hand at Sister's New York design firm; the barrel back chair and lampshades feature modern fabrics by Sister Parish Design.

Above: A pair of antique dogs were painted by Bartlett and adorned with real collars. *Opposite, clockwise from top left*: The china cabinet showcases dishes and other curiosities, while glassware from various eras is displayed in open shelves. A sketch by Sister's business partner, Albert Hadley. Shards of pottery and sea glass make for a colorful display.

Opposite: Sunshine-yellow walls and a green floor topped with needlepoint rugs make this hallway a focal point. *Above*: A daybed with an antique canopy is paired with Sister Parish Design motifs in a guest room.

Opposite and above: In a bedroom, original beadboard cladding on the walls and ceiling nods to the home's origins, while a dresser is painted the same shade as the floor. The wallcovering is a recent Sister Parish Design pattern.

Above: A red, painted bookshelf displays Dodie Thayer lettuce ware and other ceramic vegetables. *Opposite*: Photographs are among the treasures arranged on a bedroom vanity. Windows are framed by vivid, floral drapes. *Overleaf*: From the edge of the property, you can see how the home rambles—a result of various expansions over its two-hundred-year lifespan.

NANTUCKET, MASSACHUSETTS

LIVING HISTORY

In 1717, Nantucket's Proprietors of the Common—a group of English investors—laid out twenty-seven fish lots south of Main Street, between Orange Street and Pine Street. (Fish lots were so named because of their original use as sites for drying fish, which were typical of early maritime communities.) The area, located not far from Nantucket Harbor, quickly filled with residences, shops, barns, and even an oil manufactory. Only a few of these early buildings remain, one of which dates to 1746 and is now Elizabeth Markel's summer home.

A leisurely stroll from Nantucket's cobbled downtown, the shingled house, which sits on a private, narrow dirt lane barely wide enough for today's robust SUVs to amble down, is a treasure, according to Markel, an interior designer and developer who bought the house in 2016. "First and foremost, we were drawn to the home's history," she says. "There are so few houses like this on the island, or anywhere, really." When her family purchased it—their second home on the island—they were only the fourth family to own the house throughout its 270-year lifetime. While the structure had been expanded over the centuries, the original two-room floor plan was intact, and many of its early architectural elements remained. "That the house had been preserved like this was huge. Many of the older houses on the island have been transformed so much you can't tell what they were like originally," says Markel.

Opposite: Antique Nantucket lightship baskets are among the multiple collections that Markel has on display in her home; these are purse versions made of rattan and cane, with a solid wood base.

That's not to say the house was in pristine condition; in fact, it was far from it. "It was in very rough shape, beams were crumbling from beetle damage, and all the horsehair plaster had to be taken out," recalls Markel. "The house was virtually taken down to the studs. But we wanted to take the time, effort, and cost to help bring the authenticity back to it."

It was quite an undertaking, even more of a project than they'd planned on, which is often the case when it comes to restoring historic architecture. And it was expensive; Markel lovingly refers to the beloved home as her Money Pit. But the two-year process was worth it. Markel sees her family as stewards in the home's legacy. "We're only here for a short time in the home's lifespan. Our goal was to preserve the house so it could endure for another two hundred years," she says.

After leveling the foundation to accommodate a lower level of living space, which includes a fantasy bunk room with six bunks connected by bridges, hanging chairs, and plush reading nooks underneath a ceiling sheathed with constellation wallpaper, the house rose again in its original incarnation, with a few modest tweaks. In her commitment to retain the home's historic origins, Markel sought preservation-minded craftspeople to work on the project. "I was tough on them," she remembers. For example, when it came time to replaster the walls, the specialist they hired did seven rounds of test trials before they approved the materials from an authenticity perspective. "Horsehair plaster has a very specific texture, and while it's not used anymore, you can achieve a similar look. But it's not easy."

Original beams were repaired and reinstalled, while others were re-created out of salvaged wood. Floors were laid with the old wide-plank wood, exposed nails and all. The home's low ceiling heights were retained, except in the kitchen, which was relocated to connect to the new family room and patio. "We took out a bedroom upstairs to create a vaulted ceiling that makes the space feel airy and bright," says Markel, an avid cook and entertainer. She had the island topped with two-inch-thick nonmitered marble that has a distressed appearance in alliance with her ethos about the nature of the house. "It's summer, life is happening. I refuse to worry about stains or nicks."

For the pantry, Markel took cues from nineteenth-century architecture. "Back then, instead of a pantry, a home would have a larder that was more of a closed-off closet," she says. Utilizing nineteenth-century mahogany shelving that had been taken out of the library of a home she was working on in Boston, the woodwork looks straight out of Downton Abbey, installed here behind sliding pocket doors. In the same vein, she concealed a subzero wine refrigerator with an antique wood icebox. "I didn't want a stainless steel wine fridge, so I took the icebox and turned it into a skin, using it as millwork to cover the fridge."

Serious history aside, the interiors have a whimsical, relaxed livability to them—notice the powder room's glass skull sconces. "I didn't try to be historically accurate when it came to furniture because who can live like that? But I did put elements into each room that would feel timely and appropriate to what might have been in the home during different time periods," she says. There are nautical nods and elements that resonate with a country vibe, as Markel feels that the house embodies the spirit of a country home as much as it's a summer cottage located down the road from the beach.

With its verdant, tree-shrouded yard and garden—all planted by Markel—the home feels surprisingly secluded for a property close to town, and they put the privacy to good use. "We spend so much time outdoors in the summer; it's a big part of how we live in the house. We do pizza parties and chili fest where there are lots of kids running around." There's a table that accommodates twelve on the patio and there is more seating on the back porch, which has infrared heating so it's comfortable for dining through October. "But I wanted another outdoor dining space," recalls Markel, and so she had a shed constructed in the yard to hold intimate dinner parties. The space is eclectic and collected with framed vintage pictures on the ceiling and a smattering of old straw hats on the wall. "I wanted it to look and feel almost like a garage, attic-y place where all your grandmother's stuff is stored," says Markel, with a laugh. "The funny thing is that much of this stuff was actually my grandmother's. I love being surrounded by it all." The house stands as living history: weathered, whimsical, and welcoming, ready for another two hundred years of stories.

❋

Overleaf: The original living room features a piece of macramé art that Markel found at a store on the island. The freshly upholstered armchairs and trunks are antique, while the sofa is a contemporary piece.

Above: Fitted with antique shelving that was removed from a Back Bay Boston brownstone, the pantry is modeled after a nineteenth-century larder. *Opposite*: The dining room table is an old refectory table used in a monastery. Markel purchased all the vintage vessels on the sideboard from a store in Atlanta. *Overleaf left*: Arteriors Canton chandeliers hang above the kitchen island. *Overleaf right*: Vintage Cleo Baldon chairs and a banquette surround the table in the breakfast nook.

Opposite: A corner of the house was bumped out to accommodate a new stairwell that goes up to the second floor and down to the new lower level. The exposed posts and beams are original to the home. *Above*: Touches of whimsical decor abound, including this Tattoo wallpaper by Cookie Bros. and wall sconces made from skull-shaped vodka bottles, in the half bathroom.

Above: The second-floor guest room features a custom-made, arched tester bed. *Opposite*: In the primary bedroom, the bamboo-framed, decoupaged midcentury bed was expanded from a queen size to a king.

TONY DUQUETTE
Art in Time
FLOWERS CAROLYNE ROEHM

Antares
Skorpione
Taurus
A PICTURE HISTORY OF THE UNITED STATES OF AMERICA

Opposite: In the bunk room on the lower level, there are six beds connected by ladders and bridges. The ceiling is covered in Star Map wallpaper by Mr Perswall. *Above*: The adjacent bathroom features a blue-and-white trough sink with three faucets and Hex Star floor tiles by Popham Design. *Overleaf*: Markel prepares to entertain in the backyard dining shed. The ceiling art installation was inspired by Earth at Hidden Pond, a restaurant in Kennebunkport, Maine. Markel's summer centerpieces often include blooms picked from her gardens.

STONINGTON, CONNECTICUT

HISTORIC EDIT

Nestled on a mile-long peninsula that projects into Fishers Island Sound and Little Narragansett Bay, the town of Stonington, incorporated in 1662, is one of Connecticut's oldest villages. Located midway between New York City and Boston, the coastal enclave has somehow slipped under the radar as a summer haven, which suits residents—most of whom have roots stretching back decades, or even centuries—just fine. If you are lucky enough to become acquainted with Stonington's beaches and glistening harbor, its historic architecture and quintessential downtown, you'll be lured by its timeless, tranquil nature and inspired to find reasons to return.

Interior designer Kari McCabe spent the summers of her youth—living in a converted historic church filled with character, no less—in Stonington. "Growing up, summers there were idyllic. Stonington has an amazing sailing harbor," she says, noting that she and her siblings engaged in every other water sport imaginable, too. Home to a vibrant fishing community since the nineteenth century, "the downtown is very small—about a block and a half long," she says. "It essentially stopped growing in the 1800s." McCabe's husband, architect Nate McBride, began visiting the area with his wife decades ago, and likens the town to a time capsule.

While the couple shared a summer house in Stonington with McCabe's siblings for much of their marriage, eventually the creative duo craved a retreat of

Opposite: The mantel in the dining room wasn't repainted to show its history. Above the table hangs a vintage pendant by Danish brand Dog and Morup.

their own. Initially they considered building a modernist-inspired residence or a version of a modern New England barn, something simple with clean lines. "We looked and looked. We couldn't find land, and all the old houses we looked at had been significantly renovated and we didn't really want to have to undo all the work that had been done to make the place our own," says McCabe.

But there was one home they kept circling back to: a compact 1799 post and beam colonial with a symmetrical wood facade and large windows. "It wasn't what we were looking for at first, but we realized that we could make it great without a ton of work," says McCabe. Contributing to the appeal of the property was the location. About ten minutes from town, the house is surrounded by lush, verdant fields. "We're on a beautiful country road and the neighboring properties are huge farms; it's magical. All we see are cows," says McBride with a laugh. "We have dogs so the open landscape is really wonderful for them."

The previous owner had renovated the home a decade before McBride and McCabe purchased it, including the costliest updates associated with antique houses: installing new heating systems and building a new foundation. "There wasn't that much that needed to be done. We could see how with a few very deft moves we could make this house spectacular," says McCabe.

The couple's design mantra was to add nothing but rather to subtract or edit. McBride says, "It was a great exercise." The key objective was to increase the home's connectivity to the landscape. To this end, they removed a small bathroom and a wall on the main level to transform a bedroom into what the couple refers to as a "summer" living room that opens via French doors onto the large deck. "The giant deck is where we live in the summer, and it adds a whole other dimension to the house," says McCabe.

To avoid the cramped feeling created by the home's low ceilings, doorways were removed and rooms were opened to one another. "When we did this, we made sure that there was always a window wherever you are in the house," says McCabe. "That's the kind of thing that is incredibly satisfying to create." The dark, wide-plank wood floors were stained a lighter shade to help the house feel more open and brighter, and all the windows were left unadorned to incorporate the views into the aesthetic as much as possible.

Part of the editing process involved paring back elements the previous owner had installed "that were too historically correct," like the "swampy yellow, ye-olde green" painted kitchen cabinets, which are now painted in Benjamin Moore Stonington Gray. Some of the upper cabinets were swapped with open shelving, and a large pot rack was removed to keep the flow airy. A heavy dish rack in front of a window that impeded the view also went by the wayside.

"Nate allowed me to have full say in the wallpaper," teases McCabe, who filled the decor with color and pattern, much of which was influenced by her Scandinavian heritage. The dining room wallpaper is Paradiset by Josef Frank for Svenskt Tenn, and Vårklockor, another lively wallpaper from the same maker, is in the lower-level bedroom, where the doors are painted a joyous reddish-orange hue. Rugs throughout the home pop with color, too; several are made in Sweden by McCabe's Company, Mor Rugs.

"The pieces we surround ourselves with have to be comfortable and hard-wearing," says McCabe. Much of the furniture is vintage, collected over the couple's years together. Many are modernist designs, which McBride says lighten up the historic architecture. Other things are new. "It's not about stylistic consistency. There is a lot of enjoyment to be had in the dialect of the old and the new; together they animate each other," he says. Most precious are the items that have come from the couple's parents and grandparents. The Eames desk chair in McBride's office came from his parents' home, as did the George Nelson bureau in the primary bedroom. Above it hangs a gilt Italian mirror from McCabe's grandparents. There's a vintage Hudson's Bay blanket in a guest room that belonged, long before the couple met, to an old friend of McBride's.

It's a lovely assemblage of elements, accented with works by self-taught artists that the couple has been drawn to over the years. "All the pieces in the house," says McBride, "are parts of our lives." And now the house is, too.

Overleaf left: The deck is furnished with vintage wrought iron furniture.
Overleaf right: The windows have natural wood frames, while the clapboards are painted in Benjamin Moore White O1. *Pages 118–119*: McCabe's mother was a textile designer, which led to her love of hard-wearing and comfortable fabrics; the sofa is over twenty years old.

RISK
SCRABBLE

Above: The vintage kitchen table and chairs are placed next to two window walls that allow glorious views of the yard. *Opposite*: In the living room, a Danish, low-profile, leather sofa slides under the windows. Vintage armchairs are from McCabe's grandparents' home.

VIKING

Opposite: The home's existing kitchen cabinets were painted in what McCabe refers to as "swampy yellow, ye-olde green" that called for an overhaul. They're now painted in Benjamin Moore Stonington Gray. *Above*: You enter the home through the mudroom, where yellow gingham curtains from Serena & Lily hide the washer and dryer.

151-MO-1355
JAMES BALDWIN
Magnum Ireland

Opposite: A vintage Eames plywood table serves as McBride's desk in his office. *Above*: A chair found on a New York City street is nestled into a dormer window.

Above: Vintage green sconces in a bathroom play off the garden motif of the Schumacher wallcovering. *Opposite*: Quadrille Cecil wallpaper envelopes the primary bedroom. Akari ceiling lamp by Iasmu Noguchi draws the eye up, and the duvet is by John Robshaw. *Overleaf*: The lower-level bedroom is awash in color, thanks to Vårklockor wallpaper by Josef Frank for Svenskt Tenn and the orange-red door, painted in Farrow & Ball Charlotte's Locks.

CHILMARK, MARTHA'S VINEYARD, MASSACHUSETTS

PASTORAL BLISS

When Ariel Ashe was growing up, her family was the only one she knew who made the trek from New Mexico to Martha's Vineyard every summer. The family, including Ariel and her sister, Alexi, lived in Albuquerque, where their father was a builder. They came to have their place on the island essentially by accident. One year, while visiting Ashe's maternal grandparents in Salem, Massachusetts, they made an impromptu trip to Martha's Vineyard. "My parents had planned to go on a trip and leave us at my grandparents' house, but there was a hurricane so their plans changed," recalls Ashe, a designer and cofounder of AD100 firm Ashe Leandro. "Instead, we rented a house for a week in Edgartown, and my parents ended up loving it so much that they decided to buy a home on the island," says Ashe.

After spending the summer months in Edgartown for several years, Ashe's parents sought a more pastoral setting and built a home on a sheep farm up-island in Chilmark. The town, home to the working fishing village of Menemsha, is a bucolic haven of tree-lined country roads and centuries-old stone walls. Here, there are large swaths of undeveloped land, rolling meadows, and the island's most pristine beaches.

"It's my favorite place in the world," says Ashe, who was 15 when her parents built the Chilmark home. Martha's Vineyard had woven itself into the fabric of

Opposite: Puddles, the family's duck, stands atop the Moroccan tiles in the kitchen.

her being long before the family moved to Chilmark. The island has been and will always be an essential part of her.

About a decade ago, Ashe's sister, Alexi, bought the land behind her parents' house on which she planned to build a home for her family. (Ashe would later design the house for Alexi and her husband, talk show host Seth Meyers.) "I started panicking that I wouldn't find a house for myself," Ashe recalls. "I knew I needed to have a place of my own, too." Eventually, she found a spot nearby on a lush two-acre plot of sloping former farmland that was condemned; it hadn't been lived in for thirty years. "As we walked up to the house, the broker said, 'Please don't go inside.' It was that bad." But of course, she did. Though the house was unsalvageable, the setting was sublime. "I knew it was what I'd been waiting for. This was pre-Covid, and I got an amazing deal."

Ashe bought the house before she met her husband, Zach Heinzerling. Once their relationship became serious, she told him about the land she'd purchased on the island. Fortunately, Heinzerling, a Texan who'd never been to Martha's Vineyard, was on board with building a summer retreat on the island. After the couple's daughter, Agnes, was born in 2019, they broke ground on a new home where the dilapidated one had been, finishing it in August 2020 before construction prices started soaring.

The house is modeled after a small cottage with a wraparound porch and farmhouse styling that Ashe had always admired in Menemsha. "I scaled ours up to make it bigger, but it has the feel of a cozy, bucolic farmhouse," says Ashe, whose business partner, Reinaldo Leandro, collaborated on the home's design. With an exterior that evokes the local vernacular, the interior—save for some key hallmarks, like the shiplap paneling in the guest wing and entry, the nickel-gap ceilings, and the one-thousand-square-foot cedar-shingled porch—takes some global cues. "It was 2020 when we were designing the interior and I felt like we were never going to travel again," recalls Ashe, "so I incorporated pieces of the places we'd been to that we loved. I wanted the house to feel like an escape, as if coming here was a vacation." One guest room has shutters and nightstands painted in Benjamin Moore Santorini Blue, inspired by colors Ashe had seen in Greece. The kitchen's concrete red-and-white Moroccan tiles are meant to evoke an Italian cucina, while the range's plaster hood reminds Ashe of New Mexico.

Furnishings comprise an array: from eBay scores, like the laundry room's Mario Buatta chintz, to family heirlooms and antique collectibles, including Ashe's collection of silver pewter. The kitchen's eighteenth-century armoire and island are from the Brimfield Antiques Show, while the rafted pine farmhouse tables on the porch and dining room were made by Ashe's dad, and paintings by her mother hang throughout the house. The living room's upholstered pieces include Swedish antique chairs paired with one from Ruemmler, a furniture line cofounded by Ashe and Leandro. Evocative of a nineteenth-century farmhouse, most rooms feature plaster walls with no finish and wide-plank French oak floors; windows are left unadorned to capture views of the green surroundings.

The home has an ample guest suite in a separate wing, designed for friends with families to come stay with privacy. The primary suite and Agnes's bedroom are on the second floor. Ashe calls her room—where you can get a peek of the ocean—"monastic. It's so simple. It's just about the views and feeling of calm I get while looking out the window." While much of the summer is spent with friends and her extended family at the beach, on boats, or hanging out at a farm, Ashe treasures the time she, her husband, and Agnes spend quietly together at the house, where she can take in the beautiful abundance of their surroundings and their slow-paced slice of country life.

Above: In the sunroom, an antique daybed sourced from Etsy looks out to the verdant landscape. *Opposite*: The landscape design was done by Quill Teal-Sullivan of Queen Valley Farm. *Overleaf*: In the living room, the sofa is upholstered in linen, and the rug is by Beauvais. A pair of antique Swedish chairs was scored on 1stDibs.

AVANT-GARDE ART IN JAPAN

Above: Kitchen cabinets are painted pale gray, while the island is an antique Amish chopping block. *Opposite*: The dining room's lofted ceiling enhances the airy vibe. The table was made by Ashe's father.

Opposite: The laundry room has a lively, yellow-and-white checkerboard floor paired with curtains made of Mario Buatta chintz found on eBay. *Above*: A tucked-away second stairway leads to the guest quarters.

Opposite: A guest room features a bed and mirror painted in Benjamin Moore Santorini Blue—inspired by a house Ashe visited in Patmos. The curtain covering the closet is a vintage chintz. *Above*: The primary bath.

Above: There are twin beds with custom, upholstered headboards in the bedroom for Agnes, Ashe and Heinzerling's daughter. *Opposite*: In a guest room, a bed from RH features a custom headboard in a Robert Kime fabric; the quilt is by John Robshaw, who is a friend of Ashe's. *Overleaf*: The porch wraps around the house, offering a glorious view of the pastoral landscape.

EAGLE RIVER

FALMOUTH, MASSACHUSETTS

IN THE PINES

It took four years for architect Jill Neubauer to locate the right site to build her family's dream home in Falmouth, a historic town on the southwestern tip of Cape Cod. "It was a wonderful journey, but none of the lots we saw really felt like us," she says. Until one day, in the mid-1990s, when Neubauer's then-husband called her at work.

"He said he'd finally found it," recalls Neubauer, who raced to check it out. The lot, located within a canopy of large pine trees, sits on Deep Pond, one of Falmouth's pristine kettle ponds formed centuries ago from glacial deposits. "It was so overgrown; you could barely walk through it. We'd driven by the spot on our searches, but didn't realize it was a buildable lot," she says. "When I got there, we walked up this meandering hill among these huge pines that you could look through to the pond. It was true love. Right away, I said 'Yes, this is it.'"

The site of a home is the basis of the entire design, according to Neubauer. "If the site can bring forward what the people have been imagining for their home, then it's perfect alignment." As she conceived the design of this home, which she lovingly refers to as Lucky Pines, Neubauer, who grew up in the north woods of Wisconsin, was inspired by her grandparents' log cabin, located on a lake near a pine forest. It holds a special place in her heart. She took that vision of the sentimental, rustic log cabin and juxtaposed it with raw, industrial elements—which was quite innovative for 1990s residential architecture. "In our

Opposite: Canoe paddles are stashed conveniently outside the door that leads to the pond.

love relationships, a fair amount of us are vexed and in love with people who are very different from us and they bring out different things in us," says Neubauer. "In architecture, it can work the same way."

Neubauer refers to the style of the house as "modern rustic industrial." Mature pine trees, used as structural columns for the home's three floors, are paired with exposed framing and steel beams. Knotty pine contrasts with colored plaster; there are no painted walls in the house as Neubauer instead opted to used tinted plaster. "The tints were derived from site elements: green pine needles, rusty pine needles, and lake sand," she says. "When you put pigment in plaster, there is so much movement and depth and richness in its imperfections."

Just before the family was due to move into the home, a fire destroyed the structure almost entirely. But rather than see it as a tragedy—no one was hurt—Neubauer took it as an opportunity to further fine-tune the design while keeping most of the initial decisions in place. The original floors had been crafted from pitch pine trees on the property that had been cleared to build the house, and because there wasn't enough wood left to re-create them, reclaimed antique pine sourced from a local sawmill was used. "They are sealed with oil-based urethane, which creates a rich, deep amber color," says Neubauer.

Connection to the landscape is everything here. By the dining table, a glass garage door was installed so the wall can be entirely opened to the landscape. "This was before NanaWall had been invented," laughs Neubauer, who remembers calling up the garage door company with what was likely an unusual request at the time. "But the glass garage door works perfectly for what I had in mind. It stays open—with a big screen—all summer; I push it up in May and drop it back down in October." Elsewhere, floor-to-ceiling doors and windows ensure that the setting is the focal point of the home's aesthetic.

The home has a cedar-clad exterior, and there are no full-height walls on the main level. "It's one, big twenty-foot-by-sixty-foot space," says Neubauer, referring to her vision of the house as an industrial warehouse crossed with a log cabin. "The walls not reaching the ceiling allows for space to flow, it lets one know that rooms exist beyond the vertical planes, enabling one to perceive the complete envelope of the house."

"The house doesn't pretend to be anything, it just puts it all out there," says Neubauer, noting that the decor is "a little campy." Nostalgic touches abound, including the blackboard—reclaimed from an old school—that serves as the pantry wall and a message board for the family. Many years ago, Neubauer's father-in-law, a dairy farmer, drew the elevation of his farm across the top, and the sketch remains intact, a cherished hallmark. The back of the concrete fireplace, another wall of sorts, also morphed into a canvas over the years. As her kids grew up, she began clipping photos to pieces of twine strung across the length of the "wall." "I created this ever-changing photo album. Now that my daughters are grown and on their own, it's my way of keeping them close," she says.

Over time, the landscape surrounding the house has evolved to include a workshop and barn, along with a shed containing guest quarters, a chicken coop, a tree house, and a pickleball court. Not far from the raspberry bushes and the brilliant blue hydrangeas, there are frequent outdoor summer dinners for family and friends, "and now, pickleball parties," says Neubauer, referencing the property's latest addition.

Neubauer swims in the pond three days a week and frequently welcomes out-of-town guests to stay in her slice of heaven. "There is a quiet calm here," she says, recalling a friend who visits every year and doesn't want to do any of the typical summer things around the Cape. "She just wants to sit here and take in the essence. It's an elixir for people, it has been for me, and I'm very grateful."

Come summer, the population of Falmouth swells. The town is full of tourists and travelers headed to the Martha's Vineyard ferries in Falmouth Harbor and in nearby Woods Hole. But the tucked-away Lucky Pines is far removed from all that. "It's quite a sanctuary," says Neubauer with a smile. Which, after all, is just what a summer house should be.

Overleaf: A glass garage door installed by Neubauer allows the wall to be completely open in the summer. One side of the concrete wall dividing the living spaces has been fashioned into a living collage with photographs and memorabilia clipped to twine. *Page 154*: A blackboard in the mudroom is perfect for family messages. The floors are reclaimed antique pine. *Page 155*: A built-in banquette provides a cozy perch at one end of the dining table.

Welcome
Home

CAMP LOTS
FOR SALE

Above: The open stairwell, visible from the kitchen stools, serves as a compelling sculptural element. *Opposite top*: Tree trunks were used to keep the steel support beams in place. *Opposite bottom*: Plates and glassware are arranged on open shelves rather than in cabinets that would impede sight lines. *Overleaf*: Music is an essential part of life in this home; a grand piano sits near Neubauer's vinyl collection.

8

ADIRONDACK CAMPS
CEZANNE
LEONARDO DA VINCI
PEKING MUSEUM

Opposite: In the library, birch logs from the family's previous home in Vermont were used as table legs and incorporated as supports for the built-in shelves. *Above*: The walls in the primary bedroom exude a mossy shade of green that emulates the leafy landscape.

CANDLEWOOD LAKE, CONNECTICUT

LIFE ON THE LAKE

ANTICIPATION BUILDS AS YOU TRAVEL DOWN THE LONG, TREE-shrouded driveway to this dark-stained board-and-batten house on Connecticut's Candlewood Lake. Completely veiled from the street, it sits seamlessly within the wooded landscape: a veritable tree house that beckons. One step through the red painted Dutch door, and you notice, at once, that this is a sanctuary. Designed to be simple and rustic, the home's foyer is a wonderful, welcoming surprise: walls are lined with built-in shelves, bursting with books, that stretch toward the ceiling. It's an enveloping delight—punctuated by a long view of the lake at the back of the property—signaling the specialness not only of the home but also of the homeowners themselves.

A couple with three young adult sons, whose primary home is in the South, had purchased the only lot on the lake that didn't yet have a home on it. "They wanted a house they could use in the summer where you could close the door and walk away," says architect Tom Kligerman of the homeowners. The idea was to design a retreat "that was fun to be in when they were there but also simple enough that they didn't need to worry about it when they weren't."

Kligerman was brought onto the project by interior designer David Kleinberg, who had worked with the homeowners on two prior residences. "They didn't want the house to make a big statement, and the lot had restrictions for building along the edge of the lake so it couldn't be a huge house," says

Opposite: The home's cedar facade was stained a dark brown to recede into the landscape.

Kleinberg. But that suited the owners perfectly since they like spending time together; they had no interest in being spread out over multiple wings.

The intent was for the home, which is just over three thousand square feet, to be able to merge with the landscape and for it to evoke the appeal of exactly what it is—a lake house. They cleared as few trees as possible to preserve the wooded integrity of the site while ensuring that the house would have abundant views of the sparkling lake. Kligerman came up with a plan for a simple structure with two low-pitched, boxlike forms and a flat-roofed section in between. The board-and-batten exterior siding is dressed up subtly, with classical moldings and pediments. To recede into the landscape, a dark palette was settled upon. "The siding is stained dark brown, but it reads black, and the moldings are indeed black," says Kligerman, noting that the dark palette also adds a unique, dramatic energy to the house.

Inside, there are intentional hallmarks of an older house. Floors are made of reclaimed character grade oak with knots, and the ceilings in the main living space are clad with reclaimed wood boards rather than Sheetrock. "We wanted materials that wouldn't be perfect," says Kligerman. "Detailing is simple. Where there is wood paneling, it looks like it could have come from an oak tree you could find on the property."

In most rooms, views of the lake take center stage. The kitchen's double-hung, full-height windows were inspired by those in Southern houses. "Here in New England, windows typically go to the sill, but I love how they go to the floor in Southern architecture," says Kligerman.

While the family's other homes, including a contemporary high-rise in New York, have neutral palettes, Kleinberg encouraged them to incorporate more color here. "I knew they weren't going to want a big cacophony of color, but I thought we could be more playful here because of the setting," he says. Walls throughout are mostly neutral—save for the second-floor family room where the walls are painted in Benjamin Moore Van Dusen Blue—while color features on the trim, doors, and millwork. The palette centers on classic New England hues: blues and reds, and paler yellows.

Furnishings favor clean lines and modest proportions and are mostly from the mid-twentieth century, with some Arts and Crafts pieces and newer

Craftsman-inspired elements. Kleinberg's team, including lead designer Terrence Charles, designed custom upholstered pieces with refined and multidimensional fabrics, though nothing feels fussy. "It's a very user-friendly house. It was important to the homeowners that it be relaxed," says Kleinberg. In addition to the home's abundant gathering spaces, there are also plenty of spots to stretch out with a book chosen from the home's library.

Kleinberg mentions one small sticking point: he had to convince the homeowners to include a screened porch in the home's design. "I told them that a screened porch is really the essence of summer living in New England, and they gave in," he says. They've come full circle in their views now; the screened porch is one of the family's favorite parts of the home. From the airy perch within the trees, they settle in for lounging, conversations over cocktails, and meals overlooking the lake, where there's always some combination of family members paddleboarding or canoeing, and if they're not cooling off on the water, they're probably engaging in a spirited tennis match on the court just beyond the house. With its black painted ceiling and trim, it was essential that the porch have a wood floor, adds Kligerman. "Stone is sometimes used, but it's much more formal; the clunk, clunk of steps on a wood deck is a lovely, very summery sound."

Above: The main entrance is a Dutch door painted in Benjamin Moore Classic Burgundy. *Opposite*: A slightly curved room serves as both the foyer and the home's library. *Overleaf*: In the living room, furnishings include new upholstered pieces and vintage elements, such as the 1970s Danish wingback chairs.

HAIKU MOMENT
WODEHOUSE
POETRY SLAM

Above: Double-hung, full-height windows in the breakfast room ensure that the surrounding landscape is on full display. *Opposite*: Soft blue cabinets are paired with a backsplash of glazed white tiles, while the unfinished oak island adds warmth to the kitchen.

Left: Cheerful red throw pillows on the oversized custom sectional infuse the mostly blue second-floor family room with an Americana vibe. *Above*: There's a window seat in each bedroom; in this one, window treatments are made of Peter Fasano fabric.

Opposite: Board-and-batten on the wall behind the bed creates an infusion of texture that echoes the ceiling detail. *Above*: The home's reclaimed character-grade oak flooring extends into the bathrooms, where it's paired with marble and high wainscoting, painted white. *Overleaf*: After the sun sets, Visual Comfort sconces illuminate the porch, where family dinners take place around the blue Richardson Allen table.

AMERICAN CRAFTS

SEAL HARBOR, MAINE

ISLAND IDYLL

Mount Desert Island, where the "desert" is pronounced "dessert," became popular in the late nineteenth century with affluent East Coasters who came to the region to rusticate in the rural setting. Laura Keeler Pierce discovered the island fifteen years ago when she met her husband, Vassar, whose family had summered here for generations; his great-great-grandfather was one of the founders of Acadia National Park. "It's one of the most beautiful places in the world," says Keeler Pierce, a Boston-based interior designer. "It has a unique topography for New England because the mountains meet the sea."

Seal Harbor, a village on the southeastern shore of Maine's Mount Desert Island, is home to Martha Stewart's elegant summer retreat. Current seasonal residents include other notable figures who like to keep a low profile while they bask in the natural glory of this pristine part of New England. A century ago, John D. Rockefeller Jr., who donated eleven thousand acres to the nearby Acadia National Park, summered here with his wife, Abby, in a half-timbered Tudor-style mansion that they enlarged to accommodate one hundred rooms.

Keeler Pierce spent years trying to figure out how to spend more time in Seal Harbor, and just before Covid took hold, she solved the puzzle. "The general store on Main Street had been vacant for years, and it was an ideal spot to open a home furnishings shop," she says. Anchoring the seasonal trove to the location,

Opposite: Nestled into a hill, the home overlooks Acadia National Park's Cranberry Isles.

they named it Rusticator. Keeler Pierce's parents came up from South Carolina to open the shop for its first season in 2020, and they never left. "They fell in love with being here, too," she says.

Before long, her parents, who love a good home renovation project, were looking at real estate on the island. When they found a gracious 1908 stucco home nestled into a hill overlooking Seal Harbor, it seemed perfect, except for one thing. "The house is seven thousand square feet and my mom thought it was going to be too much space for them," recalls Keeler Pierce. Over dinner that evening, though, they told her parents that they'd spend summers in the house with them, sealing the deal.

Over the next two years, thoughtful adjustments were made to the historic home, which had only been owned by two other families prior, while ensuring that its original essence remained intact. Modest layout changes resulted in three distinct sections of the home: one wing—what was originally the maid's quarters—is designated for Keeler Pierce, her husband, their toddler, Percy, and their two beloved golden retrievers. Her parents' area takes up the middle of the house where the airy main living spaces and access to the sprawling porch are, and her brother has a three-bedroom wing on the other side. Each space has a separate entrance and its own kitchen, but Keeler Pierce says that the extended family isn't really living independent of one another. "We're very close and share most meals together when we're all there, but it's nice to have our own space when we need downtime," she says.

Many of those meals take place on the porch at the back of the home, overlooking the sparkling expanse of the harbor and beyond to the Cranberry Isles. "We all gravitate to the porch when we are here. In Maine, you sit outside even when it's foggy. The only time you don't go out is if it's really raining or the black flies are out," says Keeler Pierce, noting that while the footprint of the house was unchanged, the porch was the one space that was expanded in the renovation. The sizable spot has accommodated cocktails for fifty people, but it also feels intimate when it's just a couple of family members quietly lounging.

Designing the home, which isn't winterized and is used May through October, was a family affair. "I really became a designer because of my parents," says Keeler Pierce with a laugh, noting that she finally found her way into this career after forays in other fields that never felt quite right. "My dad has an incredible architectural brain; he sees things very clearly. I grew up watching him and my mom pour over architectural plans. I walked through a lot of sawdust when our houses were being renovated," she recalls. "My mom always loved designing her homes; she has a real knack for decorating."

Here in Seal Harbor, Keeler Pierce collaborated with her mother on the design of her parents' space while establishing the vibe of her own family's wing. Many furnishings came with the house—some of the pieces likely date back to the time the house was built, more than a century ago—and they strove to incorporate many of them, refreshed with new paint and other subtle fixes, into the decor. The rest of the furniture comprises a mix of new and vintage pieces. "The idea was to create a collected vibe; it's a summer house so it seems right to have pieces from different eras, with different stories attached to them," says Keeler Pierce. An abundance of color, pattern, and playfully nostalgic elements are prevalent, giving rooms a welcoming appeal. A weathered, red-and-blue lobster buoy in Percy's room is an ode to the coastal locale, while in another bedroom, vintage wooden tennis rackets on the wall are a nod to summers of a bygone era. Fabric and wallcoverings feel both fresh and timeless, and there's emphasis on heritage brands, including Sister Parish Design, in order to anchor the home to its origins.

Keeler Pierce, like the rest of her family, spends most of her time at the house on the porch. But her favorite room is the dining room—where the servants once took their meals—in the quarters she shares with her husband and son. Leafy, green wallpaper and pink throw pillows on the L-shaped banquette are paired with a small, scalloped-edged antique table that sits atop the wood floors, which are painted in a neutral checkerboard pattern. The space feels like a breath of fresh air, cheerful and modern. Yet if you narrow your eyes just a bit, the scheme could also easily be of another era—this timelessness is the beautiful essence of the home, and of the island itself.

Overleaf: In the home's main living room, the chairs by the fireplace came with the house and were reupholstered. The rug is a Brimfield Antiques Show find. The two brilliant-blue sofas complement the Willie Weston fabric of the armchairs in the foreground.
Pages 184–185: The identity of the person who painted the dining room mural, inherited with the house, remains a mystery. It depicts the local harbor and surrounding islands.

Opposite top: In the main kitchen, the backsplash is composed of handmade, botanical-inspired tiles by Douglas Watson Studio. *Opposite bottom*: In Keeler Pierce's kitchen, the Soane wallcovering has a leafy motif that corresponds with the green faux leather banquette. The back of the banquette features a vibrant Schuyler Samperton pattern. *Above*: The walls in the main kitchen are painted in Farrow & Ball Pink Ground; the rounded island in Farrow & Ball Calke Green.

Opposite: Keeler Pierce had suggested that the entire butler's pantry be painted in Farrow & Ball Cinder Rose, but her dad vetoed the idea. They compromised by using the hue only on the lower cabinets. *Above*: Rattan chairs upholstered in Cassandra Harper fabric sit in Keeler Pierce's kitchen, which opens onto a deck.

Above: Twin beds are painted in Benjamin Moore Plum Perfect, and the blankets are from Keeler Pierce's store, Rusticator. *Opposite*: In Keeler Pierce's bedroom, a Sister Parish Design pattern covers the walls. The green nightstand is from Made Goods, and atop is a lamp picked up in an antique shop that is now fitted with a Fermoie lampshade.

RUTH MOORE
THE STYLISH LIFE TENNIS
THE MAINE HOUSE II

Opposite top: Pink-hued wallpaper by Thomas Strahan was used in a small bedroom, where the bed is covered with a quilt that belonged to Keeler Pierce's husband when he was a boy. *Opposite bottom*: In a twin bedroom, beds are painted in Farrow & Ball Green Smoke, and wallpaper is Pierre Frey. The lamp on the table between the beds was made by a local potter. *Above*: An antique mirror hangs on the powder room wall amid a floral motif by Jasper. *Overleaf*: In a lavender-hued bedroom, chairs are oriented to take in the astounding view of the harbor and the islands beyond.

Opposite: The stucco and the green palette of the exterior enable it to recede into the landscape. *Above*: Signs indicate the names of past and present homeowners in the neighborhood.

WEST CHOP, MARTHA'S VINEYARD, MASSACHUSETTS

RUSTIC RETREAT

Owners of the beloved Cambridge, Massachusetts, restaurant Pammy's, Chris and Pam Willis met on Nantucket, where they both worked for years. The couple owned a cottage on the island and spent several summers there, with their two girls. "Nantucket is wonderful, but because we were [at the time] so professionally entrenched in the community, it felt like less of an escape for us," says Chris, noting that after a while, they craved more of a sanctuary, a hidden place where they could unplug entirely.

Such a retreat unveiled itself after the Willises sold their house on Nantucket, during Covid. Chris's brother and his family had recently bought land outside of Vineyard Haven, on the north shore of Martha's Vineyard. They were renovating the house on the property and asked Chris and Pam if they'd want to go in on the deal: there was over half an acre of land bordered by woods where they could build their own house. "We loved the idea. We're all very close—our kids are great friends with their cousins," says Pam. "The site wasn't perfect, but we saw the potential; we were on board really quickly."

The couple tapped Maryann Thompson, whom they'd worked with on the design of their Cambridge home as well as their restaurant, to draft the plans for the house. Design enthusiasts with a deep appreciation for craftsmanship, Pam and Chris had a pretty clear vision of what they wanted. "I was looking for the

Opposite: A deck wraps around the back of the house, overlooking the pool and the backyard.

house to feel like a camp, very lo-fi with an all-wood interior," says Chris, who envisioned a rustic experience that felt like they were all but living outdoors.

Thompson devised a pinwheel layout that maximized the home's connection to the site; rooms radiate out from the center like spokes on a wheel. Exterior spaces are nestled in between. "The plan allows for many rooms to have as many as three exposures, which is pretty unusual," says Thompson. "Most often, homes have light on two sides."

Indeed, with all the glass, "the home truly feels like an extension of the outdoors," says Pam, referencing the dining room where French doors on two sides of the room offer easy access to the pool and yard. In here, rather than using the reclaimed hemlock that sheaths the rest of the floors, walls, and ceilings in the home, they arranged green tiles in an appealing herringbone pattern. "I had this image of kids running in from the pool with wet bathing suits, standing here waiting for their sandwiches," says Pam. "With the tiles, it doesn't matter if the floor gets wet."

The house needed to be able to take a beating since they usually have a house full of extended family and friends. "We have a revolving door, people are always stopping over, and everything is always large scale. We do a lot of informal dinners and pancake breakfasts," says Pam. A professional chef, Chris usually does the cooking, an activity he relishes especially in his downtime. Of course he had a few requirements for the kitchen, such as a high-powered range. While he wanted the kitchen to be a separate space, he didn't want to be isolated from the rest of the home. So Thompson and her team devised a "ticket booth"—walls of glass windows with mullions. Between the kitchen and the dining room, the windows open—a nifty way to hand off lunch to the kids just in from the pool.

When it came to the interior design, Chris and Pam felt a deep kinship with Karie Reinertson and Laura Evans, the cofounders of Mother Studio, whose work they'd seen in *Architectural Digest*. "Chris and Pam wanted the home to be warm, cozy, and playful, but were also open to unique elements that felt riskier," says Reinertson. The couple embraced most of her and Evans's suggestions, which included the powder room's floral- and fauna-inspired tiles that the design duo painted and the stenciled motif they designed for the walls and ceiling of the breakfast nook.

"Chris and Pam have such a love for design and craft," says Evans, pointing out that most of the elements selected for the home have a sentimentality to them. "They wanted to have a story connected to the items that went into the house, for each piece to mean something. They were really tuned-in to the idea that they are creating memories and special moments for their daughters here." To ensure that the space felt deeply personal to the family, Evans and Reinerston collaborated with a slew of artisans, including quilt maker Kye and Hardy, who made the vibrant-hued bedding. When they couldn't find a sofa that suited the living room, Mother Studio conceived one in collaboration with Atelier Takagi. After reviewing dozens of fabrics, they settled on one that Reinerston describes as not conventional but playful with a 1980s flair that complements the cheeky, boat-shaped coffee table.

The kitchen cabinets are painted butter yellow, and the shiny, white floors in the primary bedroom are shellacked with multiple coats of marine paint, but the rest of the home's warm wood was left untouched. "We want the wood to take on its own age over time," says Pam, adding that an element's intrinsic nature enhances after use. "Antiques are more beautiful to us. Here, we don't care if the marble gets etched or things get damaged because we're using them and living with them. The dings make them even more special to us." The recipe is simple: it's not about perfection but about the joy of living well together.

❋

Overleaf left: Landscape architecture firm Michael Van Valkenburgh Associates worked closely with Thompson; her project manager, Doug Jack; and the Mother Studio team to ensure the property had a seamless flow between the interior and the exterior. *Overleaf right*: The custom mudroom sink is made of soapstone; the undercounter curtains are made of Walter G fabric. *Pages 204–205*: In the living room, a wood stove creates a cozy environment in the winter. Mother Studio designed the sofa in collaboration with Atelier Takagi; throw pillows are covered in Pierre Frey fabric.

THE LABYRINTH
KARL BLOSSFELDT
THE ARCHITECT'S HOME
THE MAINE HOUSE

Above: While the kitchen is a separate room, it still connects with other living spaces via glass windows. *Opposite*: Lively meals are often enhanced by someone playing the piano in the dining room. The table is Nickey Kehoe, and chairs are vintage with seat cushions made of Brook Perdigon Textiles fabric.

Right: The white oak island was made by Stauffer Woodworking, while the cabinets were designed by Mother Studio and crafted by Holmes Hole Builders. *Overleaf left*: Cabinets are painted in Benjamin Moore Bronzed Beige; counters are Carrara marble. *Overleaf right*: The breakfast nook is one of the Willises' favorite spots in the house. The bench cushion is upholstered in a Soane fabric and the window shades are made of Helene Blanche fabric. From the ceiling hangs a Noguchi pendant light.

Opposite: The bed in the guest room has a custom headboard and a quilt designed by Mother Studio and made by Kye and Hardy. The lamp is by Bennet Schlesinger. *Above*: In the upstairs hallway, a Bomma pendant light illuminates the space while creating visual appeal.

Above: The girls' bathroom features a custom vanity painted in Benjamin Moore Spiced Apple Cider, with a limestone counter. The light above the mirror is made by RBW. *Opposite*: In the girls' bedroom, a triangle window follows the roofline. Beds are from Amber Interiors, and the wall stenciling was done by Mother Studio.

Opposite: In the primary bathroom, the vanity is topped with Danby marble. The floor is sheathed in Zio & Sons + clé's octagon and bouchon tiles in weathered white, while clé's Riverbed zellige tiles were used in the shower. *Above*: In the adjoining bedroom, the floor is painted a glossy white. The Nicky Kehoe spindle chair is upholstered in a check fabric from Chelsea Textiles.

Above: Vintage Herman Miller Summer Picnic posters infuse the living area of the guesthouse with color and whimsy. *Opposite*: The back of the guesthouse features a glass wall overlooking the property.

PROVENCE STYLE

SOUTHERN MAINE

GRANNY CHIC

When the owners of this beach house in Maine became grandparents, the time was right to reimagine the beloved summer retreat they'd had for nearly thirty years. There was little color in the decor, and even though the shoreline is just fifty yards from the home, the inside felt dark. They were hoping for an unfussy interior that would lend itself to lounging, family meals, and the pitter-patter of little feet but still retain a sense of heritage and exuberance.

In swooped Lilse McKenna—an interior designer known for her layered, pattern-popping "grandmillenial" style, who had recently infused the couple's condominium with fresh florals and bold stripes. "One of the things the wife wanted was to have her Gloria Vanderbilt moment," recalls McKenna, referring to Vanderbilt's 1970s Southampton bedroom, awash in pink gingham. Indeed, this was something McKenna, celebrated for weaving pattern, color, and texture together in a modern New England way, could handle.

Before the home's infusion of check could happen, McKenna, who loves to dive into research to anchor the homes she designs to the proper time and place, hit the books. "Looking back on the plans for the house, the architecture seems to have been inspired by late nineteenth-century shingle-style houses," she says. "I wanted to build on that idea while adding charm and function."

Opposite: Decorative painter Connor Owens of SO Beaux Arts created the foyer's floor motif based on a nineteenth-century pattern that McKenna referenced in a book.

She researched nineteenth-century and early twentieth-century Maine design, exploring the region's historical decorative arts. Patterned wall stencils based on grids were common, and McKenna found one particularly appealing motif in a book. Rather than create a wallcovering based on it, she blew it up to scale and had it painted on the floor of the foyer. The original foyer was expanded by removing an awkward hallway to the guest room and fitted with much-needed storage. It is now a lovely place to stop and linger.

The red, blue, and white of the foyer floor echo the rest of the home's new color scheme, which McKenna feels exudes classic Maine. "When we tend to think of the palettes used in nineteenth-century New England, we don't realize how vibrant the paint colors were," says the designer, who included every shade of blue imaginable to avoid becoming too boring or too patriotic. Aqua, for one, makes a beautiful statement in the kitchen. "It's an unexpected color to see in kitchens," acknowledges McKenna, noting that the contractors triple-checked with her that it was the correct hue, "but it feels really special."

A new cased opening connects the kitchen to the living room, which greatly enhances the flow between the main living spaces. Doorways between rooms on the main level were made into arches, as a nod to nineteenth-century Maine aesthetics. Once the dark fir beadboard walls were enlivened with crisp coats of white paint, the choice to paint the floors followed suit. "It was important that kids could run around the house with sandy feet," says McKenna. "You can touch up painted floors every winter. But stained wood is much more work to refinish."

McKenna incorporated the homeowner's gingham request with signature flair. While the pattern is one of the home's underlying themes, it's not overwhelming in any way. "We used different scales of gingham, so it's not too preppy." Red-and-white check throw pillows pop in the sitting room, the kitchen stools are upholstered with large-scale blue-and-white gingham, and there's a teal-and-cream linen variation on a sofa in the living room, where McKenna drew in multiple patterns. "To make a room comfortable, I pull in as many layers as possible. Here, using different fabrics was also a way to incorporate different time periods," she says. She emphasizes the timeless impact of this design decision: "As tastes change, they can throw in a new pattern or a lampshade, and it won't mess up the room's equilibrium."

Other grid motifs, like the one painted on the foyer floor, repeat throughout the home. "You feel taken care of in a house when you see the thought behind something," says McKenna. In the living room, screens that slide from behind the flanking bookcases to conceal the television showcase another grid depicting folk art botanical plates. McKenna based it on a nineteenth-century piece she unearthed in the archives of the Bates College Museum of Art. The homage to decorative arts is also on display in the dining room, featuring a mural modeled after the work of famed American folk artist Rufus Porter, whose work was prevalent in nineteenth-century Maine's sprawling summer residences. While Porter's murals may have been darker and brooding, this version, created by Connor Owens, is bright and joyous, depicting tall ships afloat in a dreamy summer sea.

The screened porch was doubled in size, and it has become the family's favorite place in the home. Painted green, the tranquil space feels enveloped by the tree-shrouded setting, with the ocean unfolding straight ahead. McKenna spray-painted the family's existing wicker furniture and selected textiles in green and navy blue that tie into the coloring of the landscape. According to all family members—from the littles to their grandparents—the prime perch on the porch is the hanging daybed. In this idyllic napping spot, it's almost impossible not to nod off listening to the sounds of summer in this magical haven: the synchrony of the ocean waves, the singsong harmonies of the birds, and the rustling trees in the soothing sea breeze. It's the perfect summer escape.

Overleaf: With grey shingles and green trim, the home's exterior was devised to harmonize with the tree-shrouded landscape.
Pages 226–227: Connor Owens also created the folk-art panels that conceal the television above the couch in the living room. This couch is upholstered in an Ian Mankin fabric, while the double-sided sofa's fabric is Kravet.

LINKS TO ST ANDREWS
CHARLES M. RUSSELL

Opposite: McKenna designed the fireplace surround with river rocks and wide sanded grout to mimic the rocky beaches nearby. *Above*: The armchair's red-and-blue fabric is from Bennison Fabrics; the ottoman's green-and-white fabric is Fermoie. The rug, which evokes a quilt pattern, was a custom design.

Right: The dining room mural, by SO Beaux Arts, is a whimsical take on the Maine coastline in the style of Rufus Porter. The table is an antique, and the chairs feature slipcovers made of Les Indiennes block printed fabric.

PROUTS NECK COUNTRY CLUB
1999
PROUTS NECK COUNTRY CLUB
GOLF
2015
PROUTS NECK COUNTRY CLUB
2016
PROUTS NECK COUNTRY CLUB
GOLF
2018

Opposite: Kitchen cabinets are painted in Benjamin Moore Antiqued Aqua, while most other surfaces are white. The backsplash features hand-painted ceramic tiles by Balineum. *Above*: In the pantry, blue spatterware tiles, also by Balineum, are paired with a sink skirt fashioned from Décors Barbares fabric.

Above: The sage wall in the primary bedroom serves as a soothing backdrop for the room's array of patterns, including Matouk bedding and a chaise upholstered in spring-green-and-white Kathryn M. Ireland fabric. *Opposite top*: Blue floral patterns, including the chair's Brunschwig & Fils print, create a cozy feel in the nursery. *Opposite bottom*: The laundry is painted in Benjamin Moore Vienna Green.

Overleaf: A custom wood stain brings out the green tone in the wood trim around the windows, and the furniture was spray-painted a similar green hue. Throw pillows from Sister Parish Design, Peter Dunham Textiles, and Peter Fasano add pops of pattern.

ACKNOWLEDGMENTS

IT ALWAYS HAPPENS THE SAME WAY: I OPEN THE DOOR TO OUR HOUSE IN Falmouth, on the southwestern corner of Cape Cod, step inside, and feel it. The shift. The unspooling of whatever I was carrying. The list in my head quiets; my breath slows. In one direction, it's a short stroll to the beach. In the other, Main Street bustles with kids maneuvering ice cream cones, meandering shoppers, and vacationers clinking café glasses. But here, on our dead-end street, there's a kind of stillness that settles in the moment I arrive.

I grew up here in Falmouth. Now my husband, Mike, our son, Max, our daughter, Emma, and I spend as much of the summer here as we can. The rhythm of our time here is familiar and deeply felt: I tend to the flowers and hunt for sea glass, Mike's point of pride is the lawn, and the kids, now teenagers, are forever barefoot, going in and out of the house, never closing the door. Our goldendoodle, Harley, vacillates between deep respite, splayed out in the grass, and excited pursuit of the bunnies that infiltrate the yard.

This book began, fittingly, in Falmouth. My editor at Rizzoli, Kathleen Jayes—who also knows firsthand the power of a summer house—and I sat together in a coffee shop one day, dreaming up a book that could capture this magic. I am grateful to her for bringing *The Summer House* to life.

These homes, scattered across Nantucket, Martha's Vineyard, Connecticut, Maine, and Long Island, are more than their shingles or their sea views. They are repositories of family stories, of traditions, and of chance encounters that become rituals. They remind us that summer is not just a season but a state of mind. I remain awed by the homeowners and designers who welcomed me and trusted me to share their spaces and their stories.

To all who have ever stepped into a summer house, felt themselves exhale, and known they were home—you are why I wrote this book.

First published in the United States of America in 2026 by
Rizzoli International Publications, Inc.
49 West 27th Street
New York, NY 10001
www.rizzoliusa.com

PHOTOGRAPHY CREDITS:
Shade Degges: pp. 130, 134–147
Nicole Franzen: pp. 198, 202–219
Douglas Friedman / Trunk Archive: pp. 12, 16–31, 238
Matt Kisiday: p. 2
David A. Land/OTTO: pp. 3, 94, 98–111
Sean Litchfield: pp. 9, 178, 182–197
Erin Little: pp. 1, 4, 50, 54–55, 56–73
Pernille Loof: pp. 10, 32, 36–49, back cover
Maura McEvoy: pp. 74, 78–93
Read McKendree/JBSA: front cover, pp. 7, 112, 116–129, 220, 224–237
Jane Messinger: pp. 148, 152–161
Richard Powers: pp. 162, 166–177
Cheryl Richards: author photo

PUBLISHER: Charles Miers
SENIOR EDITOR: Kathleen Jayes
DESIGN: Celia Fuller
PRODUCTION MANAGER: Rebecca Ambrose
MANAGING EDITOR: Lynn Scrabis

ISBN: 978-0-8478-7637-2
Library of Congress Control Number: 2025947224

Printed in China
2026 2027 2028 2029 / 10 9 8 7 6 5 4 3 2 1

MIX
Paper | Supporting responsible forestry
FSC® C104723

The authorized representative in the EU for product safety and compliance is Mondadori Libri S.p.A., via Gian Battista Vico 42, Milan, Italy, 20123, www.mondadori.it

Visit us online:
Instagram: @RizzoliBooks
Facebook.com/RizzoliNewYork
Youtube.com/user/RizzoliNY